# FEASTING

# ON THE WORD OF GOD:

## 40 DAYS

### OF SPIRITUAL RELEASE

Pastor Peggy Kirkling Ratliff

ISBN978-0-9961294-0-4

Printed in USA

## Acknowledgements

I honor the Lord for trusting me with this project and giving me wisdom to complete it.

This book is dedicated to the members of Holy Trinity Outreach Ministries, where this work first began as a corporate Word fast and study, based biblically on the book of James.

I wish to express appreciation to my husband Benton Ratliff for his constant support.

To Minister Adonis Price & Cre8NOLA for designing of the cover and book layout.

To Kamil Duncan and my Chicago family for the focus group and council. To my partners and friends for their support and prayers.

**For Booking information or to order other writing by Peggy K. Ratliff please send correspondence to www.pastorpeggy.org or by email peggyratliffministries@gmail.com**

# Table of Contents

Instructions
Why the Book of James?
The Blessing of the Food
What Is Fasting and Why Should We Do It?
Biblical Instructions on Fasting
Benefits of Fasting
The Wrong Way to Fast
A Fasting Mindset

# Instructions

You're getting ready to engage in a "Word Fast" for the next 40 days. You will examine the entire Book of James. **You will read the same entire chapter daily for a week.** Each day, you will have a key Scripture from that chapter to study and meditate on the principals and apply them to your everyday life. There is space provided for you to journal your thoughts about the key scripture and how you applied it to your life. Doing this time of fasting, quiet your soul from the external noises and the many distractions that comes with your everyday life. Expect to hear from the Lord doing this time with Him. Sing praise to the Lord doing your time of discouragement or weakness will help you get through.

You are to give up one meal a day for the next 40 days. The word of God will replace that meal. You are to say grace, one has been provided for you or you may make up your own.

Even though you are on a "Word Fast", you want to feed your spiritual man as much as possible. Be aware of what you watch on TV, movies, videos. Guard your ear gate, the music you listen to, the conversations you engage in. Be sure that it is uplifting and adds inspiration to enhance this time of renewal. Even your music can help bring you in to harmony. Go out of your way to perform a kind act.

My desire is that at the end of the 40 days, you will be more in tune with the spirit of God and more disciplined in your spiritual walk by faith. The Lord will strengthen you as you go deeper in the things of God. Many times, as believers we pray faithfully, and we must apply a very important principal, meditating on the word of God. According to *Joshua 1:8 "This book of the law shall not depart out of your mouth; but you shall meditate therein day and night, that you may observe to do according to all that is written therein: for then you shall make your way prosperous, and then you shall have good success"*. There are times when we need to add fasting to our prayers. Look at *Mark 9:28 "When He came into the house, His disciples began questioning Him privately, "why could we not drive [the evil spirit] out?" And He told them, "This kind can come out by nothing but prayer and fasting."*

My prayer and desire for you doing these next 40 days is that you have a closer walk and relationship with our Lord. In Jesus name!

**We encourage those with health problems to use wisdom and consult a qualified medical practitioner before fasting.**

**Pastor Peggy Ratliff**

## Why the book of James?

The Epistle of James is one of the most practical books in the New Testament. It is the how–to book of the Christian life. It explains how things are done. James offers instruction to Christians who are experiencing problems, and he advises them about how to handle those problems God's way. The book of James points out the dangers that comes with failing to place our trust in the lord. The book is focuses on enduring the test and trials that we face in our everyday life. Topic include improper speech, bitterness, judging one another, and leaving God out of our plan. He gives us instruction on our responsibilities in our walk as a Christian. His illustration is simple, but it will take some work on our part to apply some of the concepts.

## BLESSING OF THE FOOD (the word)

Father God, as I sit down to eat your precious bread, The Word, which is life. I ask that it be nourishment and strength for my spiritual man. I give up a natural meal at this time to gain a spiritual richness. According to Colossians 3:16 *"the word of Christ dwells in me richly in all wisdom". In Jesus name, Amen*

# What is fasting and why should we do it?

Unger's Bible Dictionary explains that the word "fast" in the Bible is from the Hebrew word sum, meaning "to cover" the mouth, or from the Greek word *nesteuo*, meaning "to abstain." For spiritual purposes, fasting means to go without eating and or drinking. Read Esther chapter 4, for the Bible gives examples of God's people occasionally combining fasting with their prayers to stir up their zeal and renew their dedication and commitment to Him. Fasting is a means of getting our minds back on the reality that we are not self-sufficient. Esther know that what her people needed could come from only God and if God didn't intervene they would have perished. Fasting helps us realize just how fragile we are and how much we depend on the Lord. David humbled himself with fasting in **Psalm 35:13"** *but as for me, when they were sick, my clothing was sackcloth: I afflicted myself with fasting; and I prayed with head bowed on my breast.*

The Bible records that great men of faith fasted so that they might draw closer to God. Let's look at some of those great men. Moses in Exodus 34:28 *"And he was there with the LORD forty days and forty nights; he did neither eat bread, nor drink water. And he wrote upon the tables the words of the covenant, the Ten Commandments".* Look at Daniel in *Daniel 9:3 "And I set my face unto the Lord God, to seek by prayer and supplications, with fasting, and sackcloth, and ashes".* 2 Corinthians 11:27 Paul wrote, *"In weariness and painfulness, in watching often, in hunger and thirst, in fasting often, in cold and nakedness".* Even Jesus fasted look at *Matthew 4:2 "And when he had fasted forty days and forty nights, he was afterward hungered. Jesus knew that His true disciples, once He was no longer there in the flesh with them, at times would need to fast to regain and renew their zeal to serve Him".* James tells us, "Draw near to God and He will draw near to you" *(James 4:8)*

## Biblical instructions on fasting

*Matthew 6:16-18 Moreover when ye fast, be not, as the hypocrites, of a sad countenance: for they disfigure their faces that they may appear unto men to fast. Verily I say unto you, they have their reward. But thou, when thou fastest, anoint thine head, and wash thy face; That thou appear not unto men to fast, but unto thy Father which is in secret: and thy Father, which seeth in secret, shall reward thee openly. It even gives us instructions for married couples in 1 Corinthians 7:5 Do not deprive one another, except it be with consent for a time, that ye may give yourselves to fasting and prayer; and come together again, that Satan tempt you not for your incontinency.*

## Benefits of Fasting

Isaiah 58:6-12 The Message (MSG)

**6** "This is the kind of fast day I'm after: to break the chains of injustice, get rid of exploitation in the workplace, free the oppressed, cancel debts.

**7** What I'm interested in seeing you do is: sharing your food with the hungry, inviting the homeless poor into your homes, putting clothes on the shivering ill-clad, being available to your own families.

**8** Do this and the lights will turn on, and your lives will turn around at once. Your righteousness will pave your way. The God of glory will secure your passage.

**9** Then when you pray, God will answer. You'll call out for help and I'll say, 'Here I am.' A Full Life in the Emptiest of Places "If you get rid of unfair practices, quit blaming victims, quit gossiping about other people's sins,

**10** If you are generous with the hungry and start giving yourselves to the down-and-out, your lives will begin to glow in the darkness, your shadowed lives will be bathed in sunlight.

## The wrong way to fast

Just as there is a right way to fast, there is a wrong way to fast. Take a look at *Isaiah 58:3-5 (NIV) 3 'Why have we fasted,' they say, and you have not seen it? Why have we humbled ourselves, and you have not noticed? "Yet on the day of your fasting, you do as you please and exploit all your workers. 4 Your fasting ends in quarreling and strife, and in striking each other with wicked fists. You cannot fast as you do today and expect your voice to be heard on high.5 Is this the kind of fast I have chosen, only a day for people to humble themselves? Is it only for bowing one's head like a reed and for lying in sackcloth and ashes? Is that what you call a fast, a day acceptable to the Lord?*

## A Fasting Mindset

Daniel and Nehemiah set the example of having a repentant frame of mind look at *Daniel 9:3-4 [3] And I set my face unto the Lord God, to seek by prayer and supplications, with fasting, and sackcloth, and ashes: [4] And I prayed unto the LORD my God, and made my confession, and said, O Lord, the great and dreadful God, keeping the covenant and mercy to them that love him, and to them that keep his commandments; Nehemiah 9:1-2 [1] Now in the twenty and fourth day of this month the children of Israel were assembled with fasting, and with sackclothes, and earth upon them. [2] And the seed of Israel separated themselves from all strangers, and stood and confessed their sins, and the iniquities of their fathers.*

**Fasting also helps us learn the lessons of the need to resist Satan. Now let us draw nearer to our God by applying the scripture to our lives by fasting and praying with the word of God.**

# WEEK ONE

## SEEING THE WISDOM OF GOD IN ADVERSITIES

## James 1

## (REMEMBER TO READ THE CHAPTER SEVEN DAYS)

*James, a bondservant of God and of the Lord Jesus Christ, to the twelve tribes which are scattered abroad:*

*[2]My brethren, count it all joy when you fall into various trials, [3]knowing that the testing of your faith produces patience. [4]But let patience have its perfect work, that you may be perfect and complete, lacking nothing. [5]If any of you lacks wisdom, let him ask of God, who gives to all liberally and without reproach, and it will be given to him. [6]But let him ask in faith, with no doubting, for he who doubts is like a wave of the sea driven and tossed by the wind. [7]For let not that man suppose that he will receive anything from the Lord; [8]he is a double-minded man, unstable in all his ways.*

*[9]Let the lowly brother glory in his exaltation, [10]but the rich in his humiliation, because as a flower of the field he will pass away. [11]For no sooner has the sun risen with a burning heat than it withers the grass; its flower falls, and its beautiful appearance perishes. So the rich man also will fade away in his pursuits.*

*[12]Blessed is the man who endures temptation; for when he has been approved, he will receive the crown of life which the Lord has promised to those who love Him. [13]Let no one say when he is tempted, "I am tempted by God"; for God cannot be tempted by evil, nor does He Himself tempt anyone. [14]But each one is tempted when he is drawn away by his own desires and enticed. [15]Then, when desire has conceived, it gives birth to sin; and sin, when it is full-grown, brings forth death.*

*[16]Do not be deceived, my beloved brethren. [17]Every good gift and every perfect gift is from above, and comes down from the Father of lights, with whom there is no variation or shadow of turning. [18]Of His own will He brought us forth by the word of truth, that we might be a kind of first fruits of His creatures.*

*[19]So then, my beloved brethren, let every man be swift to hear, slow to speak, slow to wrath; [20]for the wrath of man does not produce the righteousness of God*

*[21]Therefore lay aside all filthiness and overflow of wickedness, and receive with meekness the implanted word, which is able to save your souls.*

*[22]But be doers of the word, and not hearers only, deceiving yourselves. [23]For if anyone is a hearer of the word and not a doer, he is like a man observing his natural face in a mirror; [24]for he*

observes himself, goes away, and immediately forgets what kind of man he was. [25] But he who looks into the perfect law of liberty and continues in it and is not a forgetful hearer but a doer of the work, this one will be blessed in what he does.

[26] If anyone among you thinks he is religious and does not bridle his tongue but deceives his own heart, this one's religion is useless. [27] Pure and undefiled religion before God and the Father is this: to visit orphans and widows in their trouble, and to keep oneself unspotted from the world

# DAY 1

## Meditation Scripture

James1:2 "Consider it a great joy, my brothers, whenever you experience various trials"

## Reflection - JOY VERSES HAPPINESS

These two words are used as one and the same at times, but they are actually different. Happiness is an emotion usually directly related to circumstances that are currently happening. So, when the circumstances are good and going our way, we feel happy, when things do not go our way, we feel sad and are not happy. So, you see we don't want temporary emotional happiness.

Joy is something entirely different from happiness. Joy, in the biblical context, is not an emotion. What God gives us is eternal and everlasting and must include the Holy Spirit. The word Joy here is about strength faith and belief. The Lord doesn't want you happy about trials that arise in your life. Seeing the wisdom of God in your Adversities and knowing that the joy of the lord is your strength (Nehemiah 8:10), should bring you into a place of peace that you otherwise wouldn't have. The lord wants you to have faith and believe that He's with you at all time, in good and bad time. That's Joy!!

## MEDITATION NOTES

Examine how you apply joy to the unpleasant circumstance that arise today:


**Bible verses talking about JOY:**

Habakkuk 3:17-19, Nehemiah 8:10, Galatians 5:22, Hebrews 12:2, Luke 6:23,

# Notes

_____

_____

_____

_____

_____

_____

_____

_____

_____

_____

_____

_____

_____

_____

_____

_____

_____

_____

# DAY 2

## Meditation Scripture

James 1:5 *Now if any of you lacks wisdom, he should ask God, who gives to all generously and without criticizing, and it will be given to him.*

## Reflection – WISDOM

Wisdom has to be the foundation to build upon (To build; to make; to set up; to erect; to construct). Proverbs 24:3 tell us that wisdom is a house builder and proverbs 4:7 says wisdom is supreme. Our focus verse today tells us if we lack wisdom in any area of your life ask God for it and He will give it generously. Can it be that simple? Matthew 7:7 tell us *"Ask and it will be given"*.

Remember Solomon? He asks God for wisdom, and God gave him wisdom, (1 Kings 4:29). Because Solomon asked for wisdom to understand his job to be king to discern justice and did not ask for anything selfish it pleased the Lord and He gave him so much more read 1 Kings Chapter 3. When your heart is right before God and He will hear you when you call upon Him for wisdom.

One of the best things that happen to me was James 1:5. Seeing the wisdom of God in adversities when I need wisdom the most. The harder I tried in my marriage to make it work the worse it got, then I began to pray James 1:5 for wisdom for my marriage, the Lord help me and now my marriage is strong. After today I pray you will get the wisdom you need in what you are facing. Let me impart some wisdom here, when Solomon ask for wisdom to discern justice it didn't just drop from heaven a situation occurred in 1 Kings 3:16 – 28. In your life situation may occurred to give you the wisdom you need, so pay attention! The Lord will be your guide as he was for Solomon and for me.

## MEDITATION NOTES

Today asking for wisdom when you are having trouble figuring something out or understanding something:

## Bible verses talking about WISDOM:

Job 28:28, James 3:17, 2 chronicles 1:10, Psalm 90:12

## Notes

_____

_____

_____

_____

_____

_____

_____

_____

_____

_____

_____

_____

_____

_____

_____

_____

_____

## DAY 3

## Meditation Scripture

James1:8 *"A double-minded man is unstable in all his ways"*

## Reflection – INDECISIVENESS

We are indecisive when we unable to decide or make up our mind about something. Someone who is indecisive could be constantly unsure, changing their mind often. That person has conflict going on within and need to seek the wisdom of God for His peace and guidance to make the right choices. Stand for what is right no matter the difficulties involved.

In James 1:6 double-minded is like a wave of the sea that is driven and tossed by the wind, that conflict. One who is double-minded is like someone without any anchor. This person has no discernment and is influenced by everything around them; at the end of the passage he is unstable in all his ways. We must make sure that God is our anchor especially in difficult time. How can God be our anchor?

I had to stop just reading the word of God and start studying the word of God. We read in 2 Timothy 2:15 "Study to show thyself approved unto God, a workman that need not to be ashamed, rightly dividing the word of truth". I started spending time in prayer seeking the will of God for my life and for clarity about the thing(s) that was causing me to be double-minded. Jeremiah 29:11 says "For I know the plans I have for you declare the Lord, plans to prosper you and not to harm you, plans to give you hope and a future".

It is in the midst of difficulty that your faith is tested. Remember day 2, doing difficulty time you need to ask God for wisdom, not your emotion. Seeing the wisdom of God in Adversities bring peace.

## MEDITATION NOTES

**Thank about something that you have been double-minded or unsure about and ask God for clarity:**

## Bible verses talking about INDECISIVENESS:

1 Kings 18:21, Hosea 10:2, Luke 16:13, 1 Corinthians 10:21

# Notes

_____

_____

_____

_____

_____

_____

_____

_____

_____

_____

_____

_____

_____

_____

_____

_____

_____

_____

# DAY 4

## Meditation Scripture

James1:12 *"Blessed is the man that endured temptation: for when he is tried, he shall receive the   crown of life. Which the Lord hath promised to them that love him."*

## Reflection – FIRM FAITH

*Enduring means to remain firm, as under trial to suffer patiently or without yielding; to bear up under adversity; to hold out.*

 It is in the midst of difficulty that your faith is tested. Remember Peter? when he was with Jesus he was firm in his faith, cutting the man's ear off, then telling Jesus that he would die for Him. The minute that Jesus was taken away Peter found himself lying cursing and denying he know Jesus. Sometime temptation gives us a reality check that we are not as strong as we think we are. Through temptations and trials is how the Lord shows us our strengths and weakness.

Have you ever been like Peter - Love the Lord but not strong enough to push past your fears to tell the truth because of the consequences of that truth? Well, you can sympathize with Peter because his truth may have cost him his life. He failed that test, but God always give us another chance to get it right and Peter do just that – he got it right - and you and I will do the same. When we stand firm in our faith as we are being tempted remember that the Lord will reward us even to the point of receiving the crown of life.

In *Revelation 2:10 says, "Do not fear any of those things which you are about to suffer. Indeed, the devil is about to throw some of you into prison (to trouble or stop you), that you may be tested, and you will have tribulation ten days. Be faithful until death, and I will give you the crown of life".*

Remember don't lean to your own understanding trust God's plan for your life.

## MEDITATION NOTES

What temptation has come to test you? Now how are you going to handle it?

# Bible verses talking about ENDURANCE:

Job 11:14, Job 11:15, 1 Corinthians 15:58, Matthew 10:22

# Notes

_____

_____

_____

_____

_____

_____

_____

_____

_____

_____

_____

_____

# DAY 5

## Meditation Scripture

James1:17 *"Every good gift and every perfect gift is from above, and cometh down from the Father of lights, with whom is no variableness, neither shadow of turning"*.

## Reflection – PERFECT

*Perfect means entirely without fault or defect; having no mistakes; completely correct or accurate.*

That definition does not fit myself or any one I know, what about you? There is one that fit that definition, Jesus the Son of God. John 3:16 tells us *that God so loved the world that he gives his only son.* Jesus is the perfect gift that came down from heaven of the Father. We have to receive Him as a gift and develop an understanding of the value of what we have been given. I don't have an understanding about fine art, so I can easily be fooled by a counterfeit. The gifts of Jesus are sure, when you can recognize them. Only Jesus can give you True Rest (Matthew 11:28), Keys of the Kingdom (Matthew 16:19), Power over Evil Spirits Luke 10:19), Living Water (John 4:14), Bread of Heaven (John 6:51), Peace (John 14:27), and Eternal Life (John 10:28). All seven of those gifts come from above; we just have to make ourselves available to Him to receive them.

Jeremiah 24:7 says, *"I will give them a heart to know me, that I am the LORD. They will be my people, and I will be their God, for they will return to me with all their heart"*. Luke 12:32 tells us *that it is your Father's good pleasure to bless you.*

## MEDITATION NOTES

Can you think of a few gifts that you know came from the Lord?

## Bible verses talking about BLESSING

Job 23:10; Psalm 119:67; 2 Corinthians 4:17; Revelation 7:14

**Notes**

_____

_____

_____

_____

_____

_____

_____

_____

_____

_____

_____

_____

_____

_____

_____

_____

_____

_____

_____

# DAY 6

## Meditation Scripture

James1:19 *"Wherefore, my beloved brethren, let every man be swift to hear, slow to speak, slow to wrath"*

## Reflection – LISTENING

Luke 8:18 *therefore consider carefully how you listen.* Listening requites understanding of both what is being said and what is not; (which we can see in body language, attitude, etc.). Comprehending is sometime challenging, that why your respond should be slow. Let today's meditation scripture (James 1:19) work in your life today.

Proverbs 15:2 *A wise man use knowledge rightly, but the mouth of fools pours out foolishness.* The bible tells us don't entertain a fool. Be slow to answer because sometimes silence is golden, it gives the Holy Spirit time to give you wisdom to discern or judge correctly. You do know that Satan is a deceiver and he operates in trickery using the spirit of seduction to flatter us. 1 Timothy 4:1 *Now the Spirit speaks expressly, that in latter times some shall depart from the faith, giving heed to seducing spirits, and doctrines of devils.* That is what happen to Eve in Genesis 3:13 She confessed to the Lord that she has been deceived.

There's a lot to meditate on today. Seeing the wisdom of God is needed in your listening skills. Remember proverbs 16:32 says, *he that is slow to anger is greater than the mighty; and he that rule his spirit then he that takes a city.* I myself needed the Lord help here. I talked too much so my listening skill was slow, and I was swift to speak and swift to get mad. The Lord heard me and help me, so if you find that you need help call on the Lord he is our help in time of trouble.

## MEDITATION NOTES

Will applying this scripture to your life be easy or a task?

## Bible verses talking about the TONGUE:

Psalm 34:13; Proverbs 21:23; 1 Peter 3:10; Philippians 4:8

# Notes

_____

_____

_____

_____

_____

_____

_____

_____

_____

_____

_____

_____

_____

_____

_____

_____

_____

_____

_____

## DAY 7

## Meditation Scripture

James1:26 *"If any man among you seem to be religious, and bridle not his tongue, but deceive his own heart, this man's religion is vain"*.

## Reflection – SELF CONTROL

Being religious means having or showing belief in or about God. You can be religious and never change. I was religion and I didn't have any self-control. I didn't know what was required of me as a Christian. I was deceiving myself and all that going to church was in vain because there was no change, I was not growing in the things of God. When we see the wisdom of God in our lives, then change comes. We have to hear the word and apply that word to our life. When I begin to put the word to work in my life, that's when change came.

*Psalm 141:3 set a guard over my mouth, O Lord; keep watch over the door of my lips.* That is a prayer that we all need to pray. Some think going to church or singing in the choir or maybe doing a holy dance make them religious or just doing good deed. Being religious is about change and self-control. *Luke 6:45 A good man out of the good treasure of his heart brings forth good; and an evil man out of the evil treasure of his heart brings forth evil. For out of the abundance of the heart his mouth speaks. James 3:2 if anyone is never at fault in what he says, he is a perfect man, able to keep his whole body in check.* Every time I read this I have to ask the Lord to help me and I thank Him for His grace.

## MEDITATION NOTES

What is your mouth telling you about your heart?

## Bible verses talking about SPEAKING:

Ephesians 4:31; Titus 3:1; Titus 3:2; Proverbs 11:9

# Notes

_____

_____

_____

_____

_____

_____

_____

_____

_____

_____

_____

_____

_____

_____

_____

_____

_____

_____

# Day 8

## A TIME OF REFLECTION

## SEE THE WISDOM OF GOD IN ADVERSITIES

Congratulations! you have finished the first week of your "Word Fast". Now it is time for reflection. *1 Corinthians 11: 31-32, For if we would judge ourselves, we would not be judged. But when we are judged, we are chastened by the Lord, that we may not be condemned with the world.*

## Look back at week

Were you able to see the wisdom of God in adversities doing your first week? What worked for you? What do you need to change? Did the time and place work? Did you feel yourself being drawn into the presence of the Lord at your time with your word fast? Did you read James chapter one every day doing you time with your word fast or another time worked better? Were you able to quiet your soul from the external noises and the many distractions that comes with your everyday life? Did singing praises to the Lord doing your time of discouragement or weakness help. What day was difficult for you and why? Be honest with yourself this will help your spiritual walk.

If there was a day doing the first seven days that you still needed to work on, continue to pray in that area as you move forward. Remember the more you exercise your faith and pray in this area of need, the stronger you will become. Be encourage! What kind act did you do

Remember; the 40-day word fast is designed to strengthen your faith and to develop and strength your daily walk with the Lord. There is a reason why you want the word of God to take root in your heart. *John 15:7 If ye abide in me, and my words abide in you, ye shall ask what ye will, and it shall be done unto you.*

# Notes

_____

_____

_____

_____

_____

_____

_____

_____

_____

_____

_____

_____

_____

_____

_____

_____

_____

_____

_____

_____

_____

## Week Two

# LIVING RIGHT BEFORE GOD

## James 2

*My brethren do not hold the faith of our Lord Jesus Christ, the Lord of glory, with partiality. ² For if there should come into your assembly a man with gold rings, in fine apparel, and there should also come in a poor man in filthy clothes, ³ and you pay attention to the one wearing the fine clothes and say to him, "You sit here in a good place," and say to the poor man, "You stand there," or, "Sit here at my footstool," ⁴ have you not shown partiality among yourselves, and become judges with evil thoughts?*

*⁵ Listen, my beloved brethren: Has God not chosen the poor of this world to be rich in faith and heirs of the kingdom which He promised to those who love Him? ⁶ But you have dishonored the poor man. Do not the rich oppress you and drag you into the courts? ⁷ Do they not blaspheme that noble name by which you are called*

*⁸ If you really fulfill the royal law according to the Scripture, "You shall love your neighbor as yourself," you do well; 9 but if you show partiality, you commit sin, and are convicted by the law as transgressors. ¹⁰ For whoever shall keep the whole law, and yet stumble in one point, he is guilty of all. ¹¹ For He who said, "Do not commit adultery," also said, "Do not murder." Now if you do not commit adultery, but you do murder, you have become a transgressor of the law. ¹² So speak and so do as those who will be judged by the law of liberty. ¹³ For judgment is without mercy to the one who has shown no mercy. Mercy triumphs over judgment.*

*¹⁴ What does it profit, my brethren, if someone says he has faith but does not have works? Can faith save him? ¹⁵ If a brother or sister is naked and destitute of daily food, ¹⁶ and one of you says to them, "Depart in peace, be warmed and filled," but you do not give them the things which are needed for the body, what does it profit? ¹⁷ Thus also faith by itself, if it does not have works, is dead.*

*¹⁸ But someone will say, "You have faith, and I have works." Show me your faith without your works, and I will show you my faith by my works. ¹⁹ You believe that there is one God. You do well. Even the demons believe—and tremble! ²⁰ But do you want to know, O foolish man, that faith without works is dead? ²¹ Was not Abraham our father justified by works when he offered Isaac his son on the altar? ²² Do you see that faith was working together with his works, and by works faith was made perfect? ²³ And the Scripture was fulfilled which says, "Abraham believed God, and it was accounted to him for righteousness. And he was called the friend of God. ²⁴ You see then that a man is justified by works, and not by faith only.*

[25] *Likewise, was not Rahab the harlot also justified by works when she received the messengers and sent them out another way?*

[26] *For as the body without the spirit is dead, so faith without works is dead also.*

# DAY 9

## Meditation Scripture

James 2:2-4, *For if there should come into your assembly a man with gold rings, in fine apparel, and there should also come in a poor man in filthy clothes, ³and you pay attention to the one wearing the fine clothes and say to him, "You sit here in a good place," and say to the poor man, "You stand there," or, "Sit here at my footstool, ⁴have you not shown partiality among yourselves, and become judges with evil thoughts?*

## Reflection – FAVORITISM

If we would be real with ourselves we all at one point or another in our life have judge someone wrong just by looking at them. We stereotype people, we put them in a box or in a category. If we are going to live right before God, we must follow the word in 1 John 4:1 *Beloved, believe not every spirit, but try (test) the spirits to see whether they are of God: because many false prophets have gone out into the world.* People who are sent by Satan often come in disguise. When we are living right before God we would do what the word of the Lord says in 1 Samuel 16:7 *Do not look on his appearance or on the height of his stature but look at the heart.*

Sometime the outward man would fool you; we have to look beyond that. Zechariah 3:3 *Joshua was dressed in filthy clothes as he stood before the angel*, but in verse 4, God takes away the filthy garments from him. That's what God has to do with each of us, no matter how dressed up we are on the outside. This doesn't just apply to our church services but to our everyday life. Favoritism is a sin. Pay attention to how you treat the so-called nobody's in your surroundings, they can make you somebody.

## MEDITATION NOTES

Pay attention see if you can figure out what category people have put you in

## Bible verses talking about TESTING ALL THINGS:

Jeremiah 6:27; Jeremiah 8:5; Ephesians 5:10; 1 Thessalonians 5:21

# Notes

_____

_____

_____

_____

_____

_____

_____

_____

_____

_____

_____

_____

_____

_____

_____

_____

_____

_____

# DAY 10

## Meditation Scripture

James 2:8 *"If you really fulfill the royal law according to the Scripture, You shall love your neighbor as yourself, you do well;"*

## Reflection – GODLY LOVE

Wherever there's a golden rule and you apply it to your life, it brings a blessing. If you are going to do well in this life, (living right before God) you will need the God kind of love. Jesus says in John 15:12 *"this is my commandment (golden rule), that ye love one another, as I have loved you"*. In John 13:35 *"By this shall all men know that ye are my disciples, if ye have love one to another"*. This love is unconditionally, that is the love that the father has for us. *"God so love the world that he gave his only son"*. (John 3:16)

Romans 5:8 *We read, "But God demonstrates his own love for us in this: while we were still sinners, Christ died for us"*. The God kind of love much be demonstrates. Matthew 7:12 says *"so in everything, do to others what you would have them do to you, for this sums up the Law and the Prophets"*. Galatians 6:7 tells us *"What a man sows, that shall he reap"*, think about how you treat other. James 4:11 makes it clear *"do not slander one another"*. Let us do well by loving (caring) for one another and that is living right before God.

## MEDITATION NOTES

Today is "love checkup day" see if you are demonstrating the God kind of love.

## Bible verses talking about BROTHERLY LOVE:

Deuteronomy 10:19; Matthew 22:39; 1 Thessalonians 3:12; 1 Peter 1:22

# Notes

_____

_____

_____

_____

_____

_____

_____

_____

_____

_____

_____

_____

_____

_____

_____

_____

_____

_____

_____

_____

# DAY 11

## Meditation Scripture

James2:9 *"but if you show partiality, you commit sin, and are convicted by the law as transgressors."*

## Reflection – TRANSGRESSOR

A transgresses is one who breaks a law or violates a command; one who violates any known rule or principle of rectitude; a sinner. Have you ever seen yourself as a transgressor, one who breaks the law or violates it? To violate is to fail to comply with. It is so easy to be out of comply of God's word about partiality and favoritism. We are to treat all people with respect. Remember, only God can help us though the Holy Spirit to not show favoritism, so we ask Him now for His help in Jesus' name.

The bible tells us in Leviticus 19:15, *"you shall do no injustice in judgment. You shall not be partial to the poor, nor honor the person of the mighty. In righteousness you shall judge your neighbor".* No special treatment to anyone. But 1 John 4:1 tell us "Do not believe every spirit but test the spirit to see whether they are from God". People know how to disguise themselves so in righteousness you shall judge, not based on their appearance alone. Appearance alone is truly a set up by the enemy, *"for even Satan disguises himself as an angel of light"* (2 Corinthians 11:14)

## MEDITATION NOTES

Today, see if you have been showing special treatment or have someone miss judge you

## Bible verses talking about PARTIALITY:

Deuteronomy 1:17; Job 13:10; Malachi 2:9; 1 Timothy 5:2

# Notes

_____

_____

_____

_____

_____

_____

_____

_____

_____

_____

_____

_____

_____

_____

_____

_____

_____

_____

_____

# DAY 12

## Meditation Scripture

James 2:10 *"For whoever shall keep the whole law, and yet stumble in one point, he is guilty of all"*.

## Reflection – RIGHTEOUSNESS

If we are going to live right before God, we have to know there is only one that can keep us and presence us without fault. He is the God of our salvation. Jude 1:24 *to him who is able to keep you from falling (stumbling) and to present you before his glorious presence without fault and with great joy.* Look at Isaiah 61:10, for it tells us *"the Lord has arrayed me in a robe of righteousness'.* Our righteousness is of the Lord, He gives it with great joy. Paul says in Romans 7:18, *I know that nothing good lives in me, that is, in my sinful (flesh) nature. For I have the desire to do what is good; but I cannot carry it out.* Can I tell you neither can you or I, we all need the righteousness of Christ because He was the lamb that was without spot or blemish.

We have to come to the understanding that there is no litter or big sin, sin is sin. That litter white lie is sin, that murder that we see so big is just sin. That liar is not any better than that murder and that murderer is not any better than a thief. All sin is out of the will of God. Let us stay with the Lord and learn how to live right before God.

## MEDITATION NOTES

How do you view your righteousness?

## Bible verses talking about RIGHTEOUSNESS OF CHRIST:

Isaiah 11:5; Isaiah 59:16; Je 23:5; Re 19:11

# Notes

_____

_____

_____

_____

_____

_____

_____

_____

_____

_____

_____

_____

_____

_____

_____

_____

_____

_____

# DAY 13

## Meditation Scripture

James 2:14 *"What does it profit, my brethren, if someone says he has faith but does not have works? Can faith save him?"*

## Reflection – WORKS

Your works are a direct reflection of your faith. The word of God tells us in Mark 11:22 "that we shall have Faith in God", not our own abilities. Jesus said in John 5:19 that "the Son can do nothing by himself". Jesus had faith in the father and we too, have to have faith in God. Believe on the Lord Jesus and the works that He did and we to shall do them and greater works shall we do according to John 14:12. Mark 11:23, He tell us, that if we do not doubt in our heart, but believe, we will have whatsoever we say.

When you live right before God your works will be based on having faith in God. Believe in the Lord Jesus and remove all doubt so we can produce for the kingdom. The bible says in John 15:8" this is to my Father's glory, that you bear much fruit, showing yourselves to be my disciples". In 1 Peter 2:12 we are told "live such good lives among the pagans (world) that God be glorify". Let us have works that match or look like our faith.

## MEDITATION NOTES

What have your works produce for the Kingdom?

## Bible verses talking about WORKS:

Job 37:14; Matthew 12:37; Luke 6:45; Galatians 5:19

# Notes

_____

_____

_____

_____

_____

_____

_____

_____

_____

_____

_____

_____

_____

_____

_____

_____

_____

_____

# DAY 14

## Meditation Scripture

James 2:19 *"19 You believe that there is one God. You do well. Even the demons believe—and tremble!"*

## Reflection – LOVE & OBEDIENCE

Many believe there is a God, I can remember when I believe that there was a God. I attend church regularly but didn't know too much about the God that I sang about. The devils believe and what did it produce for him? He lost his position in the kingdom. There comes a time that the Lord will deal with them that lack knowledge of Him. To know God is to love him and obey His commandments according to John 14:15. Jesus said in Luke 6:46 "why do you call me Lord, and do not what I say"?

There are people today that believe but they do not love God enough to submit unto obedience but instead rebel and reject God by refusing to walk in obedience. Look at 1 Samuel 15:22b "to obey is better than any sacrifice" and verse 23 says "for rebellion is as the sin of witchcraft, because you have rejected the word of the lord; he has also rejected you". Let us not just believe that there is a God, let us walk in obedience because we believe. The blessing is in obedience so live right before God.

## MEDITATION NOTE

If you had to rate yourself on a scale of 1-10 on obedience to God word would it be a high or low?

## Bible verses talking about OBEDIENCE:

Deuteronomy 26:16; Joshua 1:8; Matthew 7:21; Acts 5:2

**Notes**

_____

_____

_____

_____

_____

_____

_____

_____

_____

_____

_____

_____

_____

_____

_____

_____

_____

_____

_____

# DAY 15

## Meditation Scripture

James 2:20 *"But do you want to know, O foolish man, that faith without works is dead"?*

## Reflection – ACTION

"Now faith is the substance of things hoped for, the evidence of things not seen. Our faith moves us to action and without that action there can be no substance" (Hebrews 11:1). Your action can only go as few as your faith take it. If I believe God is my source, then my actions - my works - reflects my faith causes me to have evidence that I'm in faith. You have to fertilize your actions and your faith with the right words, because life and death is in the power of your tongue. A farmer can plant the seeds but if he doesn't fertilize he can lose all his hard work. You see, the word of God tells us we shall have whatsoever we say. Your words are just as important as your actions.

Don't let discouragement, worried or anxiety steal what you are believing God for. In Luke 8:14 says that the cares and riches of this world will choke the word of God. Galatians 6:9 we read, "let us not be weary in well doing; for in due season we shall reap, if we faint not". When you keep the faith, you are living right before God.

## MEDITATION NOTES

What do your actions say about your faith?

## Bible verses talking about WORKS PROVE:

Matthew 5:16; Luke 10:37; John 5:36; 1 Peter 2:12

# Notes

_____

_____

_____

_____

_____

_____

_____

_____

_____

_____

_____

_____

_____

_____

_____

_____

_____

_____

_____

_____

# Day 16

## A TIME OF REFLECTION

## LIVING RIGHT BEFORE GOD

Great! you have completed week two and now it is time for reflection.

*"Study to show thyself approved unto God, a workman that need not to be ashamed, rightly dividing the word of truth"* (2 Timothy 2:15)

## Look back at your week

At this point you should have a good routine going and quieting your spirit from the external noises and distractions should be a little bit easier. Do you feel good about the work in the word of God that you are doing? Do you find that you handle everyday situations differently since you began this study? Which lesson has helped you the most? What day was most difficult and why? What will you do differently moving forward?

Take some time and look over the lessons and your notes from the last two week. Make note of what you still need to work on as you move forward. Be encourage! Zechariah 4:10 tells us *"do not despise theses small beginnings, for the Lord rejoices to see the work begin".* You are doing great keep going. Remember to pray your way through every situation. Jesus said he could do nothing by himself in John 5:19 and neither can we.

Remember, don't just go straight to the lesson. Read the Chapter for that week every day, it is part of your time with the Lord. Say your blessing or grace over your word fast daily, just as you would a meal. Your word fast replaces that meal.

# Notes

_____

_____

_____

_____

_____

_____

_____

_____

_____

_____

_____

_____

_____

_____

_____

_____

_____

_____

# WEEK THREE

# THE POWER OF YOUR WORDS

## James 3

My brethren, let not many of you become teachers, knowing that we shall receive a stricter judgment. ²For we all stumble in many things. If anyone does not stumble in word, he *is* a perfect man, able also to bridle the whole body. ³Indeed, we put bits in horses' mouths that they may obey us, and we turn their whole body. ⁴Look also at ships: although they are so large and are driven by fierce winds, they are turned by a very small rudder wherever the pilot desires. ⁵Even so the tongue is a little member and boasts great things.

See how great a forest a little fire kindle! ⁶And the tongue *is* a fire, a world of iniquity. The tongue is so set among our members that it defiles the whole body and sets on fire the course of nature; and it is set on fire by hell. ⁷For every kind of beast and bird, of reptile and creature of the sea, is tamed and has been tamed by mankind. ⁸But no man can tame the tongue. *It is* an unruly evil, full of deadly poison. ⁹With it we bless our God and Father, and with it we curse men, who have been made in the similitude of God. ¹⁰Out of the same mouth proceed blessing and cursing. My brethren, these things ought not to be so. ¹¹Does a spring send forth fresh *water* and bitter from the same opening? ¹²Can a fig tree, my brethren, bear olives, or a grapevine bear figs? Thus no spring yields both salt water and fresh.

¹³Who *is* wise and understanding among you? Let him show by good conduct *that* his works *are done* in the meekness of wisdom. ¹⁴But if you have bitter envy and self-seeking in your hearts, do not boast and lie against the truth. ¹⁵This wisdom does not descend from above, but *is* earthly, sensual, demonic. ¹⁶For where envy and self-seeking *exist*, confusion and every evil thing *are* there. ¹⁷But the wisdom that is from above is first pure, then peaceable, gentle, willing to yield, full of mercy and good fruits, without partiality and without hypocrisy. ¹⁸Now the fruit of righteousness is sown in peace by those who make peace.

# Day 17

## Meditation Scripture

(James 3:2) *"For we all stumble in many things, if anyone does not stumble in word, he is a perfect man, able also to bridle the whole body."*

## Reflection – STUMBLE

The word "stumble" here reference to making many mistakes when we speak. The mouth speaks from the overflow of the heart, the word tells us in Matthew 12:34. When we learn to control our tongue it is then that we are in control of the situations. David know all too well that silence is a weapon we can use against the enemy. David pretended to be insane in front of Abimelech in 1 Samuel 21:13; in Psalm 34 he did not us his word to argue with his enemy but in verse 1 of Psalm 34 he said *"I will bless the lord at all times; his praise shall continually be in my mouth"*.

We have to learn how to turn a deaf ear to the enemy and turn our praise up in the midst of adversity. Psalm 39:1 David tells us, *"I have said that I would keep my way and that I would not sin with my tongue. I shall keep my mouth from evil because of the wicked who are before me"*. *"The one who guards his mouth and tongue keeps himself out of trouble"* (Proverbs 21:23).

What I am trying to say to you is that the enemy wants the wrong thing to come out your mouth. Remember if you can control your words you can control the situations. Your words have power, life and dead is in the power of the tongue. James 1:26 tells us *"if someone considers himself religious and yet does not keep a tight rein on his tongue, he deceives himself and his religion is worthless"*. There are times even when I tried to eat healthy, I must focus to make the right choices because in the storehouse there is healthy and unhealthy. In your vocabulary there are healthy and unhealthy, and we have to make the right choices.

## MEDITATION NOTES

How are you going to guard yourself from saying the wrong things?

## Bible verses talking about TONGUE RESTRAINED:

Psalm 34:13; Proverbs 13:3; 1 Peter 3:10; Proverbs 10:18

## Notes

_____

_____

_____

_____

_____

_____

_____

_____

_____

_____

_____

_____

_____

_____

_____

_____

_____

_____

# DAY 18

## Meditation Scripture

James 3:6 *The tongue also is a fire, a world of evil among the parts of the body. It corrupts the whole person, sets the whole course of his life on fire, and is itself set on fire by hell.*

## Reflection – THE TONGUE

Have your mouth ever got you in trouble? Have you ever spoken something and wonder, "where did that come from"? Could it be that our tongue is untamed? Remember day 6, *"therefore, my beloved brethren, let every man be slow to speak"* (James 1:19). If we are going to control the tongue, them slow to speak it where we need to start. Think about what you are going to say before you say it. Believe me, it is easier said than to do, but with God all things are possible. Do you remember the children's rhyme, sticks and stones will break my bones, but words will never harm me"? It was not true then and it is not true now, some word does hurt, and some word feel so good.

You can train yourself to speak life, to build up not to tear someone down. Remember life and dead is in the power of the tongue. According to Matthew 15:18, your words reveals your heart, the word tells us that as a man think in his heart so is he. Listen to what people say to you and about you because it can be revealing their heart. The word tells us what to think about in Philippians 4:8 *"Finally, brothers, whatever is true, whatever is noble, whatever is right, whatever is pure, whatever is lovely, whatever is admirable--if anything is excellent or praiseworthy--think about such things"*. Romans 14:18, *"anyone who serves Christ in this way is pleasing to God and approved by men"*. Use the power of your words wisely!

## MEDITATION NOTES

Listen to your tongue today and see if you need to make any adjustment.

## Bible verses talking about DEFILEMENT

Isaiah 59:3; Ezekiel 43:8; Mark 7:23; Hebrews 12:15

# Notes

_____

_____

_____

_____

_____

_____

_____

_____

_____

_____

_____

_____

_____

_____

_____

_____

_____

_____

# Day 19

## Meditation Scripture

James 3:8 *"But the tongue can no man tame; it is an unruly evil, full of deadly poison"*.

## Reflection - POISON

Have you ever thought about someone tongue being poison, and not just any kind of poison but deadly? Now, that is something to think about. King David know something about deadly poison in the lips of man. He prays to the Lord in Psalm 140:3 *"They make their tongues as sharp as a serpent's; the poison of vipers is on their lips'*. Who is he talking about; look at verses 1-2 *"deliver me, O lord, from the evil man; preserve me from the violent man; which imagine mischiefs in their heart continually are they gathered together for war"*. By the hand of King Saul, King David experience liar, envy, bitterness, slander, which produces the fruit of deadly poison, which can destroy the character, credit, and reputation of men. *"Their throats are open graves; their tongues practice deceit"* (Romans 3:13). You may be thinking, that could never be me. Anytime we speak negatively about a person such as, "they are never going to amount to anything", or they are not ever going to change". Instead of speaking life, we are speaking works that don't help the situation.

We need an antidote for all the negative that comes against us as poison snake bite. We need to pray as King David did, that the Lord would deliver us and keep us safe. My mother us to tell us if you can't say something good, then don't say anything at all. Has anyone said those words about you before, or have you use them yourself. The antidote is in speaking life; example ("I can see that there are so much more to who you are, you are going to be great one day"). Use the power of your word for live!

## MEDITATION NOTES

How do you handle people who never have anything good to say?

## Bible verses talking about WISE WORDS:

Proverbs 15:1-2; Proverbs 16:24; Ecclesiastes 12:11 Isaiah 50:4

# Notes

_____

_____

_____

_____

_____

_____

_____

_____

_____

_____

_____

_____

_____

_____

_____

_____

_____

_____

_____

# DAY 20

## Meditation Scripture

James 3:9 *"With it we bless our Lord and Father, and with it we curse men, who have been made in the likeness of God"*

## Reflection – LIKENESS

Have you given much thought about being made in the image of God? What does that really mean to you? Can we make the same statement that Jesus made? in John 14:9 *"he who has seen me, has seen the Father"*. Do we resemble our heavenly father like Jesus? The characteristics of the father is love, patience, long-suffering towards other, gentleness. It is though our action that his image is seen in us. James tells us *"Out of the same mouth come praise and cursing, this should not be"* (James 3:10).

We bless God by blessing one another, Matthew 22:39 tells us to *"love your neighbor as yourself"*. I don't believe that we curse ourselves out or expose our short coming, so why do we do it to someone else? The bible even tells us to *"love your enemies, do good to them who hate you, bless those who curse you, pray for those who mistreat you"* (Luke 6:27-28). God so love the world that he gave His only son. *"God demonstrates his own love for us in this: while we were still sinners, Christ died for us"* (Romans 5:8).

We are not in control of what other do, but we are in control of our response. Don't let others bring you down to their level of low living and being used by the enemy. Pray for them as the word of God tells us, bless them in whatever capacity you are able to. Then you will be using your power of words to be a blessing to someone. Choose to exemplify the image of His likeness.

## MEDITATION NOTES

How do you think that you are doing in your looking like our heavenly Father?

## Bible verses talking about DIVINE IMAGE

Genesis 1:27; Genesis 5:1; **1 Corinthians** 11:7; Psalms 8:6

# Notes

_____

_____

_____

_____

_____

_____

_____

_____

_____

_____

_____

_____

_____

_____

_____

_____

_____

_____

_____

# DAY 21

## Meditation Scripture

(James 3:16) for where you have envy and selfish ambition, there you find disorder and every evil practice.

## Reflection – SELFISHNESS

One of the requirements for following Jesus it that we must turn from our selfish ways (Matthew 16:24). If Jesus had been selfish he would have never gone to the cross and suffered and died for us. He was perfectly positioned in the father but because he was not selfish, he took off the role of dirty and put on flash that by him the world might be save.

When you look at selfish ambition, it only looks out for itself. Do you remember the mother of James and John who went to Jesus and ask him to let one of her sons set on his right hand and the other on the left? That was selfish ambition to the point that when the other disciples heard it, they were envy and moved with indignation against the two brothers (Matthew 20:20-24). Jesus knowing the evil that was festering in their hearts called them all to himself and minister to them. "Whosoever will be chief among you, let him be your servant" (Matthew 20:27).

Greatness in the kingdom is recognized by serving other not by being sever or selfish. James and John were being selfish. We learned evil produces confusion that corrupts relationships, but God brings harmony and wisdom through love. In 1 Corinthians 14:33, *"God is not the author of confusion but of peace"*. Are you using the power of your words to speak peace and harmony or confusion?

## MEDITATION NOTES

Can you think of an area that you are selfish in and what are you going to do about it?

## Bible verses talking about UNSELFISHNESS:

Genesis 50:21; Daniel 5:17; 1 Corinthians 10:33; 2 Corinthians 8:9

# Notes

_____

_____

_____

_____

_____

_____

_____

_____

_____

_____

_____

_____

_____

_____

_____

_____

_____

_____

_____

# Day 22

## Meditation Scripture

James 3:17 *"But the wisdom that is from above is first pure, then peaceable, gentle, willing to yield, full of mercy and good fruits, without partiality and without hypocrisy".*

## Reflection – PURE

Whatever **is** pure is free of any contamination; its clean, clear and unpolluted. That is the kind of heart the Lord wants us to have with one another.

Look at 1 Peter 1:22 *"Seeing you have purified your souls in obeying the truth through the Spirit unto sincere love of the brethren, see that you love one another with a pure heart fervently":* In John 13:34 Jesus announces, *"A new command I give you: Love one another. As I have loved you, so you must love one another".* According to our scripture the love of God is peaceful and gentle because it does not have hidden motives and it is without partiality. This kind of love has no favoritism. The bible tells us that the Lord have no respect of persons (he shows no favoritism or partiality). He treats everyone with respect (Romans 2:11).

Galatians 6:2 says, *"carry each other's burdens, and in this way, you will fulfill the will of the lord".* That kind of love create strength and unity among each other. That is why the bible says to put envy and strife far from you because where jealousy and selfish ambition exist, there is disorder and every evil thing according to James 3:16. When you read 1 Peter 3:8 it says, *"be like-minded, be sympathetic, love one another, be compassionate and humble".* Loving the right way is how we will have peace on earth and good will toward all men. Let us do as David did in psalm 51:10 ask the Lord to *"create in me a pure heart and renew a loyal spirit within me".*

## MEDITATION NOTES

How can you be more aware of loving God way?

## Bible verses talking about GENTLENESS:

Proverb25:21; Romans 9:22; 2 Peter 3:9; Matthew 6:14

# Notes

_____

_____

_____

_____

_____

_____

_____

_____

_____

_____

_____

_____

_____

_____

_____

_____

_____

_____

_____

_____

_____

# Day 23

## Meditation Scripture

James 3:18 *"But the fruits of righteousness are sown in peace by those who make peace".*

## Reflection – FRUITS

One of the first things God said to man was to be fruitful. Being made in the image of God fruitfulness is an attribute from God. James 1:18 *"Of His own will He brought us forth by the word of truth, that we might be a kind of first fruits of His creatures".* The fruit that you produce speaks volumes about you. Look at what the word says about us in Matthew 7:16: *"you shall know them by their fruits",* but Verse 18 says *"a good tree cannot bring forth evil fruit, neither can a corrupt tree bring forth good fruit".* In James 1:20 *"for the wrath of man does not produce the righteousness of God".* Our fruits should produce righteousness unto our Lord. Whatever you ask the father for, receiving it is based on your fruit. Take a look at John 15:16 which says, *"You have not chosen me, but I have chosen you, and ordained you, that you should go and bring forth fruit, and that your fruit should remain: that whatsoever you shall ask of the Father in my name, he may give it to you".*

The fruits of the righteous are love, joy, peace, patience, kindness, goodness, faithfulness, gentleness, self-control (Galatians 5:22-23). The fruits of corrupt will cause you to miss your inheritance of the kingdom of God. Envy, murders, drunkenness and all manner of wickedness (Galatians 5:19-21), does not produce the fruits of righteousness so that we may have the peace of God. The word tells us that every tree that do not bring forth good fruit will be cut down and cast into the fire (Matthew 3:10). The only way we can produce fruits of righteous is to abide in Jesus, he tells us in John 15:5 *"I am the vine, ye are the branches; He that abide in me, and I in him, the same bring forth much fruit; for without me ye can do nothing".*

## MEDITATION NOTES

What does your fruit say about you?

## Bible verses talking about RIGHTEOUS:

Numbers 23:10; Job36:7; Psalms 34:15; Isaiah 3:1

# Notes

_____

_____

_____

_____

_____

_____

_____

_____

_____

_____

_____

_____

_____

_____

_____

_____

_____

_____

_____

_____

_____

# DAY 24

## A TIME OF REFLECTION

## THE POWER OF YOUR WORDS

Take a deep breath, you have taken in a lot in the last three weeks now it is time for reflection. 2 Timothy 2:16 *"avoid worldly and empty chatter, for it will lead to further ungodliness"*

## Look back at your week

What have you notice different about yourself? There was a time when I was losing weight and I could not see the difference, but other people could see it. One day someone took my picture and I was able to see the difference. At first, others will notice that something is different with you. Your spirit should be quieter, and you should be experiencing a sense of peace. Do you fine that the word for a particular day was exactly what you needed? How have your speech changed?

Every week, you have had to develop and strengthened the contents of your words by allowing God to create in you a clean heart so that your action be of God. This is critical to your moving forward. In your time of reflection today spent some time with your heart, ask the lord to reveal if there is anything that should not be there and allow the Lord to remove it. Yes, it may be painful, and you may have to spend some time in healing, but it will be worth it. Examine yourselves, the bible tells us in 2 Corinthians 13:5. Transitioning and renewing the mind is never easy and there are no shortcuts. Work the word because the word works. Keep going you're almost there.

# Notes

_____

_____

_____

_____

_____

_____

_____

_____

_____

_____

_____

_____

_____

_____

_____

_____

_____

_____

_____

_____

# WEEK FOUR

# HUMBLENESS BRINGS BLESSINGS

## James 4

*Where do wars and fights come from among you? Do they not come from your desires for pleasure that war in your members?* [2] *You lust and do not have. You murder and covet and cannot obtain. You fight and war. Yet you do not have because you do not ask.* [3] *You ask and do not receive, because you ask amiss, that you may spend it on your pleasures.* [4] *Adulterers and adulteresses! Do you not know that friendship with the world is enmity with God? Whoever therefore wants to be a friend of the world makes himself an enemy of God.* [5] *Or do you think that the Scripture says in vain, "The Spirit who dwells in us yearns jealously"?*

[6] *But He gives more grace. Therefore He says: "God resists the proud,*
*But gives grace to the humble."*

[7] *Therefore submit to God. Resist the devil and he will flee from you.* [8] *Draw near to God and He will draw near to you. Cleanse your hands, you sinners; and purify your hearts, you double-minded.* [9] *Lament and mourn and weep! Let your laughter be turned to mourning and your joy to gloom.* [10] *Humble yourselves in the sight of the Lord, and He will lift you up.*

[11] *Do not speak evil of one another, brethren. He who speaks evil of a brother and judges his brother, speaks evil of the law and judges the law. But if you judge the law, you are not a doer of the law but a judge.* [12] *There is one Lawgiver, who is able to save and to destroy. Who are you to judge another?*

[13] *Come now, you who say, "Today or tomorrow we will go to such and such a city, spend a year there, buy and sell, and make a profit";* [14] *whereas you do not know what will happen tomorrow. For what is your life? It is even a vapor that appears for a little time and then vanishes away.* [15] *Instead you ought to say, "If the Lord wills, we shall live and do this or that."* [16] *But now you boast in your arrogance. All such boasting is evil.*

[17] *Therefore, to him who knows to do good and does not do it, to him it is sin.*

# Day 25

## Meditation Scripture

James 4:3 *"You ask for something but do not get it because you ask for it for the wrong reason—for your own pleasure"*.

## Reflection – Motive

Why do you ask for the things that you pray for? Think about your recent request. Was it a need in your live or something you just want? What was your motive? In Luke 15:11-32, there was a man who had two sons. The younger one said to his father, "Father give me my share of the estate, so he divided his property between the two sons. But not long after that, the younger son left the father. There are things that are designed to take you away from the father (God) and not bring you closer. The other son got his inheritance as well, but he didn't leave the father.

It is not a sin to want things. The word tells us in Psalm 84:11 that *"the Lord will withhold no good thing from those who live right"*. Look at Luke 12:32 *"for it is your Father's good pleasure to give you the kingdom"*. So, in your prayer time when you are asking for things check your motive on why you want what you are asking for. The Lord will not answer prayers that will take you away for him. Not because he's a selfish God but He know that Satan still comes to steal, kill and destroy you, but our God came that you may have an abundant live though Him (John 10:10). That younger son asks and did receives but in the end he loss it all. He humbles himself and went back home to the father and received the abundant blessing. The abundant blessing is not just money, but he was reunited back to the father (that's Love), restored to position (that's restoration), and celebrated (that's honor).

## MEDITATION NOTES

Think of a time when you prayed for something and got it, but it was not what you though

## Bible verses talking about BAD PRAYERS:

Numbers 11:15, 1 Kings 19:4, Jonah 4:3, Matthew 20:21

# Notes

_____

_____

_____

_____

_____

_____

_____

_____

_____

_____

_____

_____

_____

_____

_____

_____

_____

_____

_____

# DAY 26

## Meditation Scripture

James 4:6 "But he gives all the more grace. And so, he says, "God opposes the arrogant but gives grace to the humble."

## Reflection – GRACE

Grace is a word that we like, we like the sound of it. We like the benefit of it, it is a giving word. Look at Psalm 84:11 says He will give grace; Acts 11:23 talks about when you see the grace of God, it makes you glad; but 1 Corinthians 3:10 the Apostle Paul tell us according to the grace of God it gives him the ability to become a wise master builder. There is time when God give great grace to his people look at Acts 4:33 and it was for doing a great work. In 2 Corinthians 12:9 we find out that His grace is sufficient (enough) in our weakness.

We can conclude that grace the unmerited favor of God is powerful in our lives. There is a downside to all that grace because grace is so amazing in our lives we take it for granite at times. The Apostle Paul in Romans 6:1 tell us *"Shall we go on sinning so that grace may increase"*? But we find in Genesis 6:3 the Lord said, *"His grace will not always strive with man always"*. Let us use grace for what it was intended. That is to do for us what we cannot do for our self's. For we are save by Grace, we are kept by grace and we are thankful for grace. Stay humble because God give grace to the humble and He withhold it from the proud.

## MEDITATION NOTES

How have you seen grace work in your live?

## Bible verses talking about GRACE:

Ecclesiastes 10:12; Malachi 1:9; Ephesians 1:7; 2 Peter 3:18

# Notes

_____

_____

_____

_____

_____

_____

_____

_____

_____

_____

_____

_____

_____

_____

_____

_____

_____

# DAY 27

## Meditation Scripture

James 4:7 *"Submit yourselves therefore to God. Resist the devil, and he will flee from you"*.

## Reflection – SUBMISSION

To yield your will or authority to another person is submission. There are two forces at work in our lives. We have to choose whether we submitted to God or follow the desires of the flash. Our desires come to bring pleasure for a season, but destruction in the end, read Proverbs 14:12.   When we resist the thoughts or the temptation that comes from the devil to do things that are not pleasing to God and don't bring Him glory, it is then that we are honoring God in submission.

If you look at the word of God in Romans 7:23 you will see the struggle of the Apostle Paul," *but I see in my body a different principle waging war with the Law in my mind and making me a prisoner of the law of sin that exists in my body"*. I like the Apostle Paul because he let us know that he is saved and love the Lord, but he still has struggles that he is dealing with. You and I have struggles as well but the good news is if we submit those struggles to the Lord He will give us the strength to resist the devil or those thoughts that come.

I can remember struggling in my personal life with smoking, I want to quit but it wouldn't quit me. I can remember calling out to the Lord for help and he give me this scripture James 4:7 *"resist the devil and he will leave you"*. I had to learn how to submit to the Lord. I can remember just saying help me Lord and the more I ask for help the Lord was with me and give me the strength to stop. When we submit ourselves to the Lord we give him permission to help us. Humbleness through submission always brings the blessing.

## MEDITATION NOTES

In what area of your life do you need the Lord's help to resist a thought or action?

## Bible verses talking about RESISTING:

Ephesians 4:26; Ephesians 4:27; 1 Peter 5:8; 1 Peter 5:9

# Notes

_____

_____

_____

_____

_____

_____

_____

_____

_____

_____

_____

_____

_____

_____

_____

_____

_____

# DAY 28

## Meditation Scripture

James 4:9 *"Let there be tears for what you have done. Let there be sorrow and deep grief. Let there be sadness instead of laughter, and gloom instead of joy"*

## Reflection – CHANGE

I can remember a time when I was out of the will of God and bragged about it to my friends. Even worse, I was proud of the things I was doing and thought I was getting away with something. When you come into the knowledge of God and His word of truth, you are coming into His marvelous light and then we are able to see ourselves as He sees us. My heart was sad when God show me myself and I was godly sorry and ask Him to forgive me of my sin and I needed His help to do better.

When change comes to our lives it is then that we give Him glory. Change only comes though confession or admitting we need to change. According to 1 Peter 2:9 *"He called us out of darkness into His marvelous light"*, because we are God's special possession. Change is never easy when someone decides to make the changes necessary to turn their lives around, it usually takes the help of others. In this case we can call on the names of the Lord and ask other to pray for us until change comes. I know it was the prayers of other that help brought me through.

The bible says in James 5:16 *"the prayers of the righteous accomplish much"*. James 4:8 tell us *"to come near to God and he will come near to you. Wash your hands, you sinners, and purify your hearts, you double-minded"*. When we read Ephesians 4:20-24 it tells us to learn about Christ and put off the former conversation of the old man, which is corrupt. And be renewed in the spirit of your mind. And put on the new man, which after God is created in righteousness. Remember Galatians 6:9 let us not be weary in well doing, for in due season we shall reap, if we faint not.

## MEDITATION NOTES

What do you need to change? Why do you need to change it?

## Bible verses talking about Spiritual Cleansing:

Isaiah 1:16; Jeremiah 4:14; Acts 22:16; 1 John3:3

# Notes

_____

_____

_____

_____

_____

_____

_____

_____

_____

_____

_____

_____

_____

_____

_____

_____

_____

_____

_____

_____

# DAY 29

## Meditation Scripture

James 4:10 *"Humble yourselves in the Lord's presence, and he will exalt you"*.

## Reflection – PROMOTION

Promotion is something we want to achieve in our life. Many strive for it by working really hard, trying to prove to their superior that they're doing a good job. When you have done your best and someone else gets the promotion, you feel like that promotion should have been yours. When that happen, life does not seen to be fair. You have to remember the word tells us that the world take care of their own in John 15:19. Be encouraged, God has a plan and we see in His word that promotion come neither from the east, nor from the west, nor from the South. In Psalm 75:6 According to Matthew Henry's Concise Commentary, he does not mention the North, the same word that signifies the North, signifies the secret place. The secret place where the Lord's plan unfolds for your life. Matthew 6:6 says, *"For what you do in secret, God will reward you openly"*. Let me clarify by looking at Colossians 3:23 *whatsoever ye do, do it with all your heart, as to the Lord, and not unto men"*. Ephesians 6:7, reads similarly; *"Serve wholeheartedly, as if you were serving the Lord, not people"*. We want our promotion to come from God and not man, you see, if man exalt you he also can take it back. Allow God to promote you in due season for the word says in Luke 14:11 *"for everyone who exalts himself the Lord will humbled, and he who humbles himself the Lord will exalted"*. There is a blessing in being humbles and doing your best at all times.

## MEDITATION NOTES

How different would your work ethic be, if the Lord was your boss?

## Bible verses talking about GOD EXALTING:

Genesis 45:8; 1 Samuel 2:7; 2 Samuel 7:8; Daniel 2:21

# Notes

_____

_____

_____

_____

_____

_____

_____

_____

_____

_____

_____

_____

_____

_____

_____

_____

_____

_____

# DAY 30

## Meditation Scripture

James 4:16 *"Otherwise you are boasting about your own plans, and all such boasting is evil"*.

## Reflection – BOASTING

When we boast about our accomplishment, we take the credit for ourselves for how God had blessed us. Psalm 52:1 ask the question, *"Why do you boast all day long, you are a disgrace in the eyes of God"?* As much as Oprah Winfrey has accomplished at the close of her talk show she made this statement and I'll never forget it: "it has been by the grace of God that I've been able to do all of this". She did not come out every show and say 'Oh God did it one more time' no! But when it matters most she gave God the credit. Giving the Lord thanks for what He does in our life is good but showing gratitude comes from a place in your soul of gratefulness. That place in us that knows if the Lord wouldn't intervene we wouldn't been able to accomplish what we have accomplish and still need to accomplish.

The bible says that He is a present help in time of need (psalm 46:1). David in Psalm 124:2-5 David describes what it would have been like if the Lord had not been on our side, when men came against us. The Lord has great things in store for us, but we must give Him the credit that is due Him. The word of God tells us in Matthew 5:16 *"let your light shine before others, that they may see your good deeds and glorify your Father in heaven"*. God's way is humble, not boasting, and is done with a grateful heart.

## MEDITATION NOTES

What are some things you could not have accomplish without the Lord?

## Bible verses talking about THANKFULNESS:

Deuteronomy 8:10; Psalm 100:4; Colossians 1:12; 1 Thessalonians 5:18

# Notes

_____

_____

_____

_____

_____

_____

_____

_____

_____

_____

_____

_____

_____

_____

_____

_____

_____

_____

# DAY 31

## Meditation Scripture

James 4:17 *"Therefore to him that knows to do good, and does it not, to him it is sin"*.

## Reflection – REBELLING

When someone says you are rebelling or rebellious, let's look at what they are saying, you are disobedient, insubordinate, unruly and wayward. This is not how we want to be identified. We represent our Heavenly Father. He expects us to operate in the spirit of excellence. Our scripture today tells us if we know to do well, then it is required of us. There is time when we know the right thing to do but we choose not to do it. We give ourselves excuses, and some of them are really good excuses. The word of the Lord tear down all of our excuses for not doing our best.

We all remember Joseph. His brothers sold him into slavery (Genesis 37:28), but everywhere that Joseph went he did his best and the Lord was with him according to Acts 7:9. If anyone had an excuse to rebel it was Joseph, but instead of rebelling he gave his best. Look what he tells his brothers in Genesis 45:8 *"So then, it was not you who sent me here, but God. He made me father to Pharaoh, lord of his entire household and ruler of all Egypt"*. As always what the enemy mean for your bad God turn it around for your good.

Always do your best, because the Lord is looking. Luke 6:35 *"love your enemies, and do good, and lend, hoping for nothing from them; and your reward shall be great, and ye shall be the children of the Highest; for he is kind unto the unthankful and to the evil"*. Remember in Matthew 5:16 Jesus tells us, *"let your light so shine before men, that they may see your good words, and glorify your Father which is in heaven"*. Don't give other people the power to stop you from doing well, because they refuse to do right. Your blessing is in doing your best.

## MEDITATION NOTES

How have this lesson help you, to want to do your best?

## Bible verses talking about REBELLING:

Deuteronomy 9:35; Matthew 7:26; Matthew 25:27; James 2:14

# Notes

_____

_____

_____

_____

_____

_____

_____

_____

_____

_____

_____

_____

_____

_____

_____

_____

_____

_____

# DAY 32

## A TIME OF REFLECTION

## HUMBLENESS BRINGS BLESSINGS

You have made it to the end of Week Four.  Now it is time for reflection. Colossians 3:10, says that we, *"have put on the new man that is renewed in knowledge after the image of him that created him"*.

### Look back at your week

As you began to look back and reflection over your week you will find that the lessons are design for you to be a better person in your walk with the Lord. When we humble ourselves to be more like the Lord, being renewed in the knowledge of him, it is then that the blessings come. Do you see yourself thinking about how to handle situations in a way that God can be seen thought your life? How are you handling negative people now? What are you doing to let your light of Christ shine more? What significant change have you seen in your life?

As you move to the final week, remember that this time with the Lord has been designed to increase your knowledge and understanding of how significant you are to your heavenly Father, and to show you that what you do matters. You increase the world for good or you add to the bad. Colossians 3:12 *"Therefore, as God's chosen people, holy and dearly loved, clothe yourselves with compassion, kindness, humility, gentleness and patience"*.

# Notes

_____

_____

_____

_____

_____

_____

_____

_____

_____

_____

_____

_____

_____

_____

_____

_____

_____

_____

_____

_____

# WEEK FIVE

# SHOWING BROTHERLY LOVE

## James 5

*Come now, you rich, weep and howl for your miseries that are coming upon you!² Your riches are corrupted, and your garments are moth-eaten. ³ Your gold and silver are corroded, and their corrosion will be a witness against you and will eat your flesh like fire. You have heaped up treasure in the last days. ⁴ Indeed the wages of the laborers who mowed your fields, which you kept back by fraud, cry out; and the cries of the reapers have reached the ears of the Lord of Sabaoth⁵ You have lived on the earth in pleasure and luxury; you have fattened your hearts as in a day of slaughter. ⁶ You have condemned, you have murdered the just; he does not resist you.*

*⁷ Therefore be patient, brethren, until the coming of the Lord. See how the farmer waits for the precious fruit of the earth, waiting patiently for it until it receives the early and latter rain. ⁸ You also be patient. Establish your hearts, for the coming of the Lord is at hand.*

*⁹ Do not grumble against one another, brethren, lest you be condemned. Behold, the Judge is standing at the door! ¹⁰ My brethren, take the prophets, who spoke in the name of the Lord, as an example of suffering and patience. ¹¹ Indeed we count them blessed who endure. You have heard of the perseverance of Job and seen the end intended by the Lord — that the Lord is very compassionate and merciful.*

*¹² But above all, my brethren, do not swear, either by heaven or by earth or with any other oath. But let your "Yes" be "Yes," and your "No," "No," lest you fall into judgment.*

*¹³ Is anyone among you suffering? Let him pray. Is anyone cheerful? Let him sing psalms. ¹⁴ Is anyone among you sick? Let him call for the elders of the church, and let them pray over him, anointing him with oil in the name of the Lord. ¹⁵ And the prayer of faith will save the sick, and the Lord will raise him up. And if he has committed sins, he will be forgiven. ¹⁶ Confess your trespasses to one another, and pray for one another, that you may be healed. The effective, fervent prayer of a righteous man avails much. ¹⁷ Elijah was a man with a nature like ours, and he prayed earnestly that it would not rain; and it did not rain on the land for three years and six months. [18] And he prayed again, and the heaven gave rain, and the earth produced its fruit.*

*[19] Brethren, if anyone among you wanders from the truth, and someone turns him back, [20] let him know that he who turns a sinner from the error of his way will save a soul from death and cover a multitude of sins.*

## DAY 33

## Meditation Scripture

James 5:4 *"Look! The wages you failed to pay the workers who mowed your fields are crying out against you. The cries of the harvesters have reached the ears of the Lord Almighty".*

## Reflection – GREED

Whenever I hear the word "greed", I think of never enough or always needing more or never satisfied. People who have a greedy mindset always lose more then they gain. The bible says in Proverbs 11:24 *"Give freely and become wealthier; be stingy and lose everything"* and in Proverbs 15:27 we read, *"The greedy bring ruin to their households, but the one who hates bribes will live'.* God's way of increasing us is foolish to the world (1 Corinthians 1:27). Giving to someone that is less fortunate than you, look what Proverbs 19:17 says, *"whoever is kind to the poor lends to the Lord, and he will reward them for what they have done".* If God has blessed you to have a business or to be able to hire someone to do a job for you be fair with them because we find in Galatians 6:7 *"Do not be deceived, God is not mocked; for whatever a man sows, this he will also reap."*

Remembering the words, the Lord Jesus in Acts 20:35 *"It is more blessed to give than to receive".* For a long time, I didn't understand that scripture. I though receiving was a blessing, the revelation the Lord give me was that He can only multiply what you give. God is looking for a generous heart that will show brotherly love like the one in Proverbs 11:25 *"A generous person will prosper; whoever refreshes others will be refreshed."* Luke 6:38 *"Give, and you will receive".* Your gift will return to you in full, pressed down, shaken together to make room for more, running over, and poured into your lap. The amount you give will determine the amount you get back." Hebrews 13:5 Keep your lives free from the love of money and be content with what you have, because God has said, "Never will I leave you; never will I forsake you."

## MEDITATION NOTES

Look for ways to be a blessing to other.

## Bible verses talking about Benevolence:

Proverbs 22:9; Isaiah 58:10; Malachi3:10; 2 Corinthians 9:6

# Notes

_____

_____

_____

_____

_____

_____

_____

_____

_____

_____

_____

_____

_____

_____

_____

_____

_____

_____

_____

# DAY 34

## Meditation Scripture

James 5:8 *"Be you also patient; establish your hearts: for the coming of the Lord draws near."*

## Reflection – BEING READY

When one is ready, they are prepared. We prepare for many things in this life, but how prepared are we for the next life? "What next life?!" you may be asking. The one where you get to see your heavenly father, the one who made you, who we have been praying to and believing that He would answer those prayers. There are times we hear someone say the Lord is coming back, as true as that may be, for many have already exit this life. When we are prepared we live every day as if it was our last.

In chapter 38 of Isaiah, we read that there was a man name Hezekiah. He was sick and near death. The Lord told Isaiah the Prophet to tell Hezekiah set his house in order, for he was going to die. Hezekiah didn't loss heart. He turned his face to the well and prayed to the Lord. How many times has a doctor said to someone that there is nothing they can do for them and give them a death sentence? But just a little talk with the Lord can make it alright. Listen to Hezekiah prayer, *"remember now, O Lord I pray, how I have walked before you in truth and with a loyal heart and have done what is good in your sight."* What a beautiful testimony of a well lived life before the Lord. What prayer would you pray if you were given a bad report from the doctor? The Bible says that the Lord added fifteen years to Hezekiah life. When you Live right before the Lord, it will always add years to your life and cause you to be ready.

## MEDITATION NOTES

How are you living this life to live again?

## Bible verses talking about READINESS:

Matthew 25:10; Mark 13:35; Luke 12:5; Luke 12:36

# Notes

_____

_____

_____

_____

_____

_____

_____

_____

_____

_____

_____

_____

_____

_____

_____

_____

_____

_____

_____

# DAY 35

## Meditation Scripture

James 5:10 *"As an example, brethren, of suffering and patience, take the prophets who spoke in the name of the Lord."*

## Reflection – EXAMPLE

Having examples in your life and in your walk of faith is very important. If there were no examples or people that has gone before us, then we would not know what to expect. In Psalm 34:19 *"many are the afflictions of the righteous, but the Lord delivers him out of them all"*. Who better to make this statement then David, who was constantly running for his life. He makes this statement in verse 8, *"O taste and see that the Lord is good, blessed is the man that trust in him."*

The Apostle Paul tells Timothy in 2 Timothy 3:11 *"the sufferings and persecutions he endured but the lord rescued him from all of it"*. Look what he says in Romans 8:18 *"yet what we suffer now is nothing compared to the glory he will reveal to us."* Paul Calls our suffering "light afflictions", yes, light afflictions. (They are not light to us but to our God). That is why those who have gone before us says that the Lord deliver them. The Prophet of old suffered much because of their righteousness. When you read the word of God, you fine that they stone many of the prophets and they didn't want to hear the truth, the word of God. Daniel was put in the lion's pit, because he was righteous again, we see that the Lord delivered. The point I'm trying to make is that you and I will have some troubles but just like those that when before us, our God will deliver us too, Matthew 5:12 tells us to *"Rejoice and be glad."*

## MEDITATION NOTES

Think about one difficult thing you went through and how the Lord delivered you from it.

## Bible verses talking about SUFFER:

Acts 7:52; Romans 5:3; Philippians 1:29; Hebrews 11:33

**Notes**

_____

_____

_____

_____

_____

_____

_____

_____

_____

_____

_____

_____

_____

_____

_____

_____

_____

_____

# DAY 36

## Meditation Scripture

James 5:12 *"But above all, my brethren, do not swear, either by heaven or by earth or with any other oath; but your yes is to be yes, and your no, no, so that you may not fall under judgment."*

## Reflection – INTEGRITY

I look at many definitions of integrity, many of them define integrity as one having good character, or principle. The one that stood out the most to me was 'the state of being whole and undivided'. What that says to me is, when you are saying yes with you lips, you are also saying yes with your heart, all of you being in agreement. Jesus said, *"these people honor me with their lips, but their hearts are far from me"*, in Matthew 15:8. That is why the Lord said in 1 Samuel 16:7 *"The Lord does not see as man sees, man looks on the outward appearance, but the lord looks on the heart"*.

Your honesty measures the depth of your Integrity. Have you heard the saying that your word is your bond? When you keep your word, people can true you. You also have to be reliable, people have to be able to count on you to do what you said you would do. When we deal truthfully with one another, God is please. Proverbs 12:22 says; *"Lying lips are abomination to the Lord, but they that deal truly are his delight."* Your heart reveals the true you, look at proverbs 23:7, *"as a man thinks in his heart, so is he, eat and drink, he says to you, but his heart is not with you."*

Integrity is not just what you say but what you do. When you have integrity, you do what is right when other are looking and when no one is looking. To many time we want to look good in the eyes of people, so we put on a mask, but we have to be true to ourselves because the Lord said *"you are the ones who justify yourselves in the eyes of other, but God knows your heart"* The disciples prayed in Luke 16:15. *"Lord, you know everyone's heart. Show us which of these two you have chosen."* That should be our prayer too that we ask the Lord to reveal the heart of people and even our own heart.

## MEDITATION NOTES

Pay attention to what your heart is saying about your integrity.

# Bible verses talking about THUTHFULNESS:

Proverbs 12:19; Zechariah 8:16; Malachi 2:6; Ephesians 4:25

## Notes

_____

_____

_____

_____

_____

_____

_____

_____

_____

_____

_____

_____

_____

_____

_____

_____

# DAY 37

## Meditation Scripture

James 5:13 *"Is anyone among you in trouble? Let them pray. Is anyone happy? Let them sing songs of praise."*

## Reflection – PRAYER

Where there is trouble or sickness, there also much be prayer. It is our responsibility to call on the Lord in our time of need. Look at Psalm 91:15, where the lord says *"when you call to me, I will answer you. I will be with you in trouble; I will deliver you, and honor you".* The Lord honor us when He answer our call and deliver us out of the situation that we find ourselves in. I have discovered that you don't need a lot of words when you are praying to the Lord, sometime "Help me, Lord" is all that is needed.

Jesus says, when you pray do not keep on babbling like some people, for they think they will be heard because of their many words". When we pray it is by faith that we believe the Lord will answer our prayers. Our prayers say to the Lord that we true Him to have a plan for the situation. Even in our own lives we turn to people that we can trust. Another reason why it is good to pray, God will always exceed our expectation. Ephesians 3:20 tells us, *"the Lord who is able to do exceedingly abundantly above all that we ask or think",*

We do ourselves an injustice when we don't pray. Do you remember the woman in Luke 8:43 that had a sickness for twelve years and spent all her money on physicians? They could not heal her, she came to Jesus after all her money was gone and was heal by him because she finally prayed. What if she had prayed twelve years ago? Prayer produce results. Great breakthroughs come with the prayer of faith. We show brotherly love when we pray one for another because prayer is never selfish. Galatians 6:2 *"carry each other's burdens."* In this way you will follow Christ's teachings.

## MEDITATION NOTES

How has the Lord exceeded your expectations in prayer?

## Bible verses talking about HEALING:

Psalm 41:4; Isaiah 53:5; Hosea 6:1; Revelation 22:2

# Notes

_____

_____

_____

_____

_____

_____

_____

_____

_____

_____

_____

_____

_____

_____

_____

_____

_____

_____

# DAY 38

## Meditation Scripture

James 5:17 *"Elijah was a human being like us, and he prayed earnestly that it would not rain and there was no rain on the land for three years and six months!"*

## Reflection – ORDINARY

When I think of Elijah, the last thing that come to mind is "ordinary". Here we have a man that the bible said he prayed that it would not rain and there was no rain for three years and six months. What makes Elijah special is that he humbled himself, so the Lord can use him. How many of us the Lord is just waiting to use, could I had done what Elijah did, just speak what we hear. The Lord say even when it doesn't make sense to us.

Think about this, you were ordinary, but once the Lord use you then you are no longer ordinary. You now are someone the Lord can use to make a difference in the world. Peter got out of the boat and walked on water because Jesus told him to come. He was just an ordinary man that believe he could, because Jesus said he could. God take our weakness and give us his strength, in 2 Corinthians 12:10 Paul says, *"when I am weak, then I am strong"* Joel 3:10 tells us to make this confession; *"let the weak say, "I am Strong".* Can you see that it is not man's ability, but it is God's ability working through man? I believe you would agree with me that Jesus was anything but ordinary. Look at the words Jesus uses in John 5:19 *"The son can do nothing of himself".* Likewise, we can only do what the Lord allow us to do though His ability. *"God has chosen the foolish things of the world to shame the wise,"* 1 Corinthians 1:27. Look at verse 26, *"for consider your calling, that there were not many wise according to the flesh, not many mighty, not many noble".* With God ability you are able.

## MEDITATION NOTES

Can you think of a time when you were weak, and the Lord intervene?

## Bible verses talking about DIVINE POWER:

Matthew 14:20; Matthew 17:27; John 2:7; Mark 4:39

# Notes

# DAY 39

# Meditation Scripture

James 5:19 *"My brothers, if anyone among you wanders from the truth and someone brings him back"*

# Reflection – LIFEGUARD

A lifeguard is an expert swimmer trained to rescue other swimmers in trouble. They are both swimmers, but the lifeguard is a trained swimmers whose job is to watch and protect those in his area from drowning. Being a spiritual lifeguard, you have to be spiritual sensitive to the needs of other. Being a lifeguard in the natural or spiritual, you cannot be selfish or biased, you are called to help who ever have a distress call in your area. Drowning people or people in trouble sometimes cannot call out for help, that is why you must be sensitive and trained to know the quiet signs of trouble.

The bible tells us in Proverbs 11:30 that *"he that win soul is wise"*. There are times in life we will need a spiritual lifeguard. When we can't see the truth clearly and we get in trouble or off course. Spiritual training comes from the Lord and when that happen you are no longer just a life guard you have become a fisherman for the Lord read Matthew 4:19. A fisherman much be patience to pray a person though and to wait on the Lord for change. To be a watchman for the lord is a privilege and we are blessed when we get to be use. Paul in 1 Corinthians 9:19 *"though I am free and belong to no one, I have made myself a servant to all that I might win more"*. We are called to save others even pulling some out of the fire according to Jude 23. You will be rewarded for your good deed, this is what Daniel had to say in Daniel 12:3 *"those who are wise will shine like the brightness of the heavens, and those who lead many to righteousness, like the stars forever"*. Showing true brotherly love is knowing how to take care of other.

# MEDITATION NOTES

Are you your brother's keeper?

# Bible verses talking about SELFFISHNESS:

Proverbs 16:8; Ezekiel 34:18; Matthew 25:43; Matthew 27:3;

# Notes

_____

_____

_____

_____

_____

_____

_____

_____

_____

_____

_____

_____

_____

_____

_____

_____

_____

_____

_____

# DAY 40

## A TIME OF REFLECTION

## SHOWING BROTHERLY LOVE

Congratulation you have made it to the end of your 40 days of spiritual release, now it is time for reflection. Genesis 4:9 ask the question, "am I my brother's keeper?" Yes, we are our brother's keeper. Jesus said to Peter *"when you are converted strengthen your brothers"* (Luke 22:32).

Now that you have feast on the word of God for 40 days share your experience with someone, so that they may be strengthen through your testimony.

## Notes

_____

_____

_____

_____

_____

_____

_____

_____

_____

_____

_____

_____

_____

# REFLECTION OF YOUR 40 DAYS

As you began to look back over the last five weeks and reflect, you will find that the lessons are design for you to be a better person in your walk with the Lord.

In Week One, "Seeing the wisdom of God in Adversities" we learn that all things do work together for our good. I didn't say it would feel good, but it will work out for your good. Remember joy verses Happiness, ask for wisdom. You don't want to be indecisive. Don't yield to temptation. Be sure to listen for understanding. Work on self-control.

In Week Two, "Living right before God", we learn that faith without works is dead. You need faith and your works are a direct reflection of your faith. As we live right before God, remember no favoritism. Showing Godly love. Our righteousness is of the Lord You will do great work for the Lord. Love the Lord and walk in obedience and take action.

Week Three, "The power of your Word". Life and dead are in the power of your tongue. Speak life to every situation that comes in your life. You will stumble and make mistakes. The tongue will get you in trouble, it is like poison. Remember, you are made in the likeness of the Lord. Do not be selfishness. Our fruit should remain.

Now Week Four says, "Humbleness Brings Blessings" The Lord gives grace to the humble and where there is grace, you will find mercy. If you have grace and mercy, you will have God's favor. Monitor your motives. God's grace is available to you. Stay in submission to the Lord. Be willing to change. Promotion comes from the Lord. Don't boast selfishly. Don't be rebellious against the truth.

Finally, we come to Week Five, "Showing brotherly love" We have to learn to live in harmony with one another, so much so that the bible says, "to love your neighbor as yourself, and to carry each other's burdens, even our enemies. The Lord tells us to do good for them. Be a giving, don't be greed. Be ready, be an example, have integrity. Pray. The Lord uses ordinary.

Remember as you move forward that this time with the Lord was designed to increase your knowledge and understanding of how significant you are to your heavenly Father and what you do matters. You increase the world for good or you add to the bad.

# YOUR THOUGHTS MOVING FORWARD

_____

_____

_____

_____

_____

_____

_____

_____

_____

_____

_____

_____

_____

_____

_____

_____

_____

_____

_____

_____

# ABOUT THE AUTHOR

Peggy Ratliff is a Pastor, Author and Teacher. As a Mentor and trainer, she is fueled by a passion to help many people find hope and restoration through knowledge.

Her candid communication style allows her to mentor and teach openly about her life experiences, so that others may apply what she has learned to their lives. She walks closely in ministry with her husband Benton Ratliff, currently serving as the Pastor of Holy Trinity Outreach Ministries in Metairie Louisiana.
She is the mother of two daughters and grandmother to six grandkids.

Peggy Ratliff conducts conferences, seminars and workshops, teaching from her published writings "Simple Instructions of Prayer" and "Feasting On The Word of God".

Pastor Peggy intends to help individuals discover an intimate relationship with God through prayer and relationship